27.99
B10.

TEEN STRONG

Wildlife Conservation WITH

Robert Irwin

by Kristy Stark

FAST READS

full tilt PRESS

Robert Irwin
TEEN STRONG

Full Tilt Press
42964 Osgood Road
Fremont, CA 94539
readfulltilt.com

Full Tilt Press publications may be purchased for educational, business, or sales promotional use.

Editorial Credits
Design and layout by Sara Radka
Edited by Renae Gilles
Copyedited by Nikki Ramsay

Image Credits
Getty Images: Alenast, background (eucalyptus pattern), ASTRA Awards/Brendon Thorne, 12, Australia Zoo, 6, Australia Zoo/Ben Beaden, 10, 15, Bradley Kanaris, 24, colematt, 26 (bottom), Discovery, Inc./Monica Schipper, cover (main), 1, 18, 27 (bottom), ElenaLux, background (Australian pattern), EyeEm/Sarayut Thaneerat, 29, EyeEm/Songsak Wilairit, 25, Frazer Harrison, 27 (top), GlobalP, 13, 23, Jon Kopaloff, 21 (bottom), Justin Sullivan, 8, 9, Lisa Maree Williams, 14, Matt Roberts, 9, nomis_g, 17, Pool/Mick Tsikas, 16, 20; Newscom: MEGA/A Carlile, 3, MEGA/AFF-USA/Tammie Arroyo, 4, Rafael Ben Ari, 19, Splash News, 7, 22, ZUMAPRESS/Globe Photos, 26 (top); Pixabay: OpenClipart-Vectors (bubble frame), pen_ash, cover (koala); Wikimedia: Aheba_Also, 21 (top), Bernard DUPONT, 11

ISBN: 978-1-62920-841-1 (library binding)
ISBN: 978-1-62920-853-4 (ePub)

CONTENTS

Introduction

What is one way to make late-night host Jimmy Fallon squeal like a toddler? Put a millipede on his hand, of course! On April 30, 2019, Robert Irwin did just that. He was a guest on *The Tonight Show*, and he brought some interesting creatures with him. His purpose was to introduce unique **species** and to educate Fallon and the audience.

Not all of the creatures made Fallon uncomfortable. Robert also brought out a baby miniature horse named Li'l Sebastian. Robert let Fallon feed the animal a bottle of milk. Robert explained that this type of horse is important to people. It is often used as a **service animal**. The horse licked Fallon's face after it ate. Robert laughed and smiled as the audience applauded.

This was the 12th time Robert has been a guest on *The Tonight Show*. Each time, he has brought amazing **wildlife** with him.

....

species: a group of plants or animals with similar features

service animal: an animal trained to assist a human who has a disability

wildlife: animals living in the wild

Getting Started

Steve had a love for reptiles from a young age. He passed this passion on to Robert.

Robert Clarence Irwin was born in Buderim, Queensland, Australia. His birthday is December 1, 2003. He is a dual citizen of Australia and the United States. His dad, Steve, was born in Australia. His mom, Terri, was born in Oregon in the US. Since his parents are from different countries, Robert is a citizen of both places.

Robert made his media **debut** at the age of one month old. In the video, his dad was holding him while feeding a large crocodile. This scene was met with much **controversy**. Many people did not think his dad should have a baby around the animal. But from that point on, Robert has spent much of his life in front of the camera. And he is usually seen with animals.

Steve wanted Robert to be comfortable around animals. He said, "I am teaching him to be completely familiar with crocodiles."

The Australia Zoo was opened in 1970 by Robert's grandparents Bob and Lyn Irwin. Their son, Steve, became known as the Crocodile Hunter due to his work with these creatures.

debut: the first time someone does something in public, such as appear on TV

controversy: strong disagreement about something

The Crocodile Hunter aired from 1996 to 2004. Terri was in many episodes alongside Steve.

In His Father's Footsteps

Long before Robert was in the spotlight, his father, Steve, was known for his love of animals. On his Animal Planet show, *The Crocodile Hunter*, Steve came face-to-face with unusual wildlife. He studied deadly snakes, lizards, spiders, and crocs. The TV star became famous for interacting with animals that people are usually afraid of. Steve showed the world that all creatures are important and should be cared for.

Robert grew up around the creatures his dad highlighted on his show. He grew up on the show too. But when the boy was two years old, his dad died. This event prompted the Irwin family to carry on Steve's important work.

Robert's family works at the Australia Zoo. He and his sister, Bindi, grew up at the zoo learning about and working with animals. They were **homeschooled** by tutors at the zoo. First they did their studies. Then they helped take care of the animals.

Since Robert was a young boy, a big part of his career has been speaking to the media. He often talks to news reporters.

STEVE IRWIN

Steve Irwin was known for handling some of the world's deadliest and creepiest beasts. Yet he was killed by a creature that is normally safe and docile. In 2006, Steve was snorkeling in Australia. He was filming a segment for a new show. He was struck in the chest by a stingray's tail and died. But his love and care for wildlife is carried on by his family.

homeschool: to learn at home instead of at a school

Becoming Teen Strong

At age 8, Robert fed freshwater crocodiles in public for the first time at the Australia Zoo. He told the media, "It was so fun, it's absolutely awesome."

obert Irwin was so young when his dad died that he does not have clear memories of him. But he does help to carry on his father's work. The teen shows people creatures they may not have seen or heard about. Robert teaches people how to care for many animals too.

Robert loves all creatures, from the cute and soft to the wild and rough. In fact, the animals that he loves the most are saltwater crocodiles. He likes them because these creatures are at the top of the **food chain**. He says they are one of the most **vital** species in an **ecosystem**. When the crocs are healthy, it is a sign that the other creatures and plants in the area are healthy too.

Saltwater crocodiles are the largest of their kind. On average, males are 17 feet (5 meters) long and weigh 1,000 pounds (450 kilograms).

Robert loves to take photos of wildlife. His love of photography started when he was six. His photos have been shown in galleries and magazines around the world.

food chain: a list of living things in which each one uses the lower member on the list as a source of food

vital: very important

ecosystem: everything that exists in a certain environment, including soil, rocks, water, plants, and animals

TV Star

In 2015, Robert started co-hosting the show *Wild But True* on Discovery Kids. The show highlights ways to protect and care for nature. It teaches people how problems are solved in the wild. The hosts explore how these solutions can help humans take better care of the planet.

In 2017, Robert started a series of appearances on *The Tonight Show Starring Jimmy Fallon*. His first time on the show, he brought a sloth for Fallon to hold. The show's audience fell in love with Robert. He is charming and intelligent, like his dad. They loved the critters he brought too.

Robert has since been on the show many more times. One of the most watched episodes involves Fallon's guest Kevin Hart. Hart was scared of each animal Robert brought out. He even ran off the stage! Over time, Robert has shown Fallon a baby camel, kangaroos, black bears, and many other animals.

In 2015, Terri and Robert attended Australia's ASTRA Awards, which honor accomplishments in TV. Steve won in 2007 for Favourite Male Personality.

IN DANGER

Robert works to protect cheetahs in Africa. Cheetahs are one of the most recognized creatures on Earth. But they are in danger of disappearing from the world. As more people live in their **habitat**, there is less room for cheetahs to roam and find food. So they eat farmer's livestock, such as goats and sheep, to survive. Farmers want to protect their animals. They trap and shoot the cheetahs. The number of cheetahs has decreased over the years.

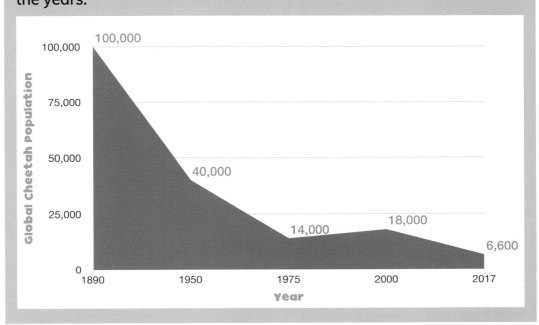

habitat: a place where a plant or animal normally lives

Wildlife Warrior

As famous TV personalities, Robert and his mom, Terri, attend many special events. In 2019, they went to Australia's ARIA Music Awards.

obert Irwin is both a TV host and a zoologist. Zoologists study wildlife and their natural habitats. They also study the ways that animals are affected by humans.

Robert studies many creatures, including those from his home country, Australia. He works to introduce people to these living things. The teen also tells people about animals that are **endangered** around the world. He educates people on how to help protect them.

Unfortunately, some of Robert's favorite beasts are already **extinct**—dinosaurs! He loves to study and learn more about them. At age nine, he co-created a series of books about dinosaurs. The series is called *Robert Irwin: Dinosaur Hunter*. In the fictional books, he has encounters with some of his favorite dinosaurs. The books share his love of these creatures, as well as facts about them.

Robert learned how to work with animals, including crocodiles, from staff at the Australia Zoo. This included Josh Ruffell, the zoo's head of reptiles when Robert was young.

About 90 percent of animal species from Australia don't live in the wild anywhere else in the world. Some of these animals are the koala, dingo, and kangaroo.

endangered: rare and in danger of dying out completely

extinct: when all the members of a species have died

In 2018, the Irwins attended a meeting about coral. Australia's Great Barrier Reef is the largest coral reef system in the world. The meeting included politicians, business leaders, and other concerned citizens.

A Family Affair

Robert does not work with and study animals on his own. Instead, it's a family affair! Robert's mom Terri and sister Bindi work with him. Together they help people better understand wildlife. They also bring attention to causes that protect creatures.

The family has a foundation called Wildlife Warriors. Its purpose is to fund projects that help wild animals. For example, they lead a project that tracks and researches crocodiles in Australia.

Habitat loss is the greatest threat to animals and plants. Steve Irwin once said, "I believe our biggest issue is the same biggest issue that the whole world is facing, and that's habitat destruction."

Another project works to protect and treat injured and sick koalas. Koalas' natural habitats are being destroyed to make room for roads and homes. This leaves the animals without homes, food, and protection.

The group also works to raise awareness about endangered rhinos. Some people hunt rhinos for their horns. This kills the rhinos. If **poaching** does not stop, they may become extinct.

Robert and his family want to protect all wildlife. They educate people about the animals. They hope people will give money to causes that help the creatures.

poach: to hunt illegally

The northern white rhino is almost extinct due to poaching. The southern white rhino is doing well, thanks to protection efforts.

Work in Progress

Animal Planet threw a party to celebrate the start of *Crikey! It's the Irwins* in October 2018. The show would go on to have 36 million viewers around the world, a record for Animal Planet.

obert continues to work closely with his family. In addition to working at the Australia Zoo, they also work together on a TV show. In 2018, Robert, his mom, and his sister began filming a show for Animal Planet. It's called *Crikey! It's the Irwins*. "Crikey" is an Australian **expression** that means "wow." His dad made it world famous. On the show, the trio highlights wildlife from around the world. The series focuses on their continued commitment to "protect wildlife and wild places."

The first season of the show was a huge success. Animal Planet approved a second season, which began in fall 2019. Season two featured the family as they completed projects around the Australia Zoo. For the 50th anniversary of the zoo, they built a new home for the crocs. Robert was tasked with moving all the crocs to their new home.

The Australia Zoo covers more than 1,000 acres (400 hectares). It is home to more than 1,000 animals.

The Irwins' Animal Planet show airs in more than 205 countries and territories, including the United States.

expression: a word or phrase

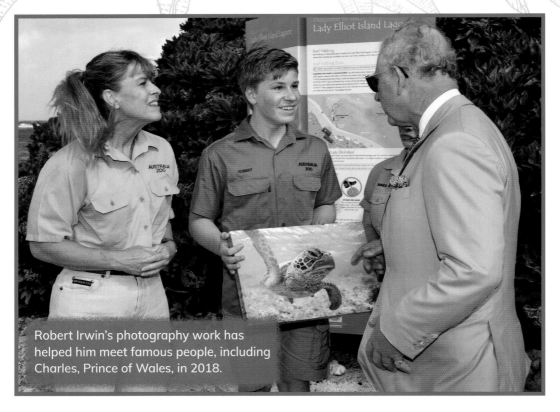

Robert Irwin's photography work has helped him meet famous people, including Charles, Prince of Wales, in 2018.

Wildlife Photography

Robert continues to take photos around the world. Most of his photos showcase wildlife and natural settings. He has won several awards for his photos. They are often used in the Australia Zoo's magazine, *Crikey*. His photos have also been sold to raise money for Wildlife Warriors.

Robert helps to run the zoo too. He often plays a role in the daily shows at the zoo. The teen especially loves to share what he knows about crocs. Robert recently shared a photo of himself feeding a croc named Murray. The shot was posted next to a photo of his dad. His dad was feeding the same croc 15 years earlier!

Robert regularly posts wildlife and scenic photos on Instagram. He has about 2 million followers. But he does not care about fame. The teen cares about keeping up the message and work his dad started. He and his entire family focus on protecting wildlife. They work to bring attention to these creatures.

Robert photographs wallabies, which are related to kangaroos.

BINDI IRWIN

Bindi Irwin has spent much of her life in the spotlight too. She became the tourism **ambassador** for Australia at age eight. With that job, she helped to promote the land and wildlife. By age nine, she had her first TV series, *Bindi: The Jungle Girl*.

Over the years, she has appeared in many shows and movies. In 2015, she was on *Dancing with the Stars*. She took home the top prize. After that, she got right back to work **advocating** for wildlife and the planet.

ambassador: someone who represents a group while living in another country

advocate: to publicly support

A Bright Future

Every year, Robert helps celebrate Steve Irwin Day at the Australia Zoo on November 15.

Robert keeps busy. He films TV shows, takes photos, and works at the zoo. He plans to continue these tasks as well as wildlife **conservation** projects in the future. The teen hopes to one day run the Australia Zoo. But for now, he learns as much as possible around the zoo and through his online studies. Robert has even had a teacher who travels with him. This has helped him stay on top of his education.

One of his favorite times of the year is the croc research trip. Every August, Robert and his team spend over a month on the river. They spend time detecting tagged crocs in the area. They place satellite trackers on new crocs they find too. This allows them to check on the creatures. The team is able to study and track the animals all year. Robert looks forward to each year's trip.

KIDS CHOICE AWARDS

Robert and Bindi won the Nickelodeon Kids' Choice award for Favorite Duo in 2018. They thanked the kids who voted for them. The siblings used the platform to encourage wildlife conservation. They reminded everyone that kids can change the world.

conservation: the protection of something, such as animals and plants

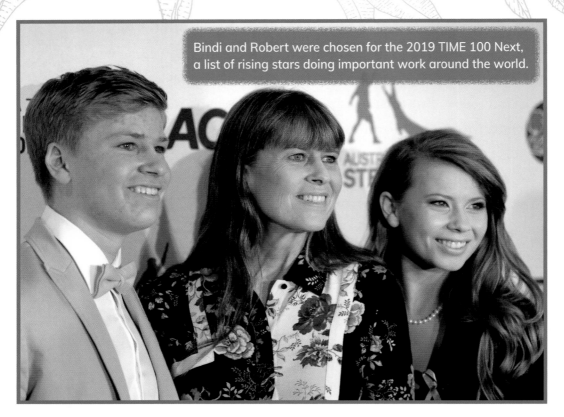

Bindi and Robert were chosen for the 2019 TIME 100 Next, a list of rising stars doing important work around the world.

Wildlife Defender

Robert Irwin is Teen Strong because he defends wildlife and nature. His entire life has been devoted to protecting the world's creatures. Robert has done this by educating people. The teen has shown people that animals considered to be dangerous are still vital to our world. Robert has shared ways to protect and care for all animals. He has also proven to be strong and brave by handling many creatures, both big and small.

Robert lost his dad at a young age. But he has worked hard to carry on his dad's work. The teen does so with a huge smile, a warm laugh, and a deep knowledge about animals.

While he shares many projects with his family, Robert has made a name for himself. His photography and appearances on *The Tonight Show* have helped him express his interests to the world. They have helped Robert draw the attention of his own fans too.

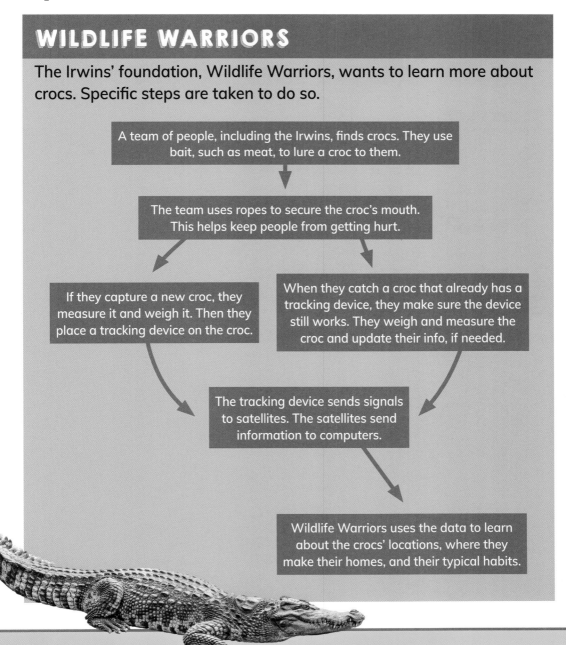

WILDLIFE WARRIORS

The Irwins' foundation, Wildlife Warriors, wants to learn more about crocs. Specific steps are taken to do so.

A team of people, including the Irwins, finds crocs. They use bait, such as meat, to lure a croc to them.

The team uses ropes to secure the croc's mouth. This helps keep people from getting hurt.

If they capture a new croc, they measure it and weigh it. Then they place a tracking device on the croc.

When they catch a croc that already has a tracking device, they make sure the device still works. They weigh and measure the croc and update their info, if needed.

The tracking device sends signals to satellites. The satellites send information to computers.

Wildlife Warriors uses the data to learn about the crocs' locations, where they make their homes, and their typical habits.

Timeline

1970

The Australia Zoo is opened by Robert's grandparents, Bob and Lyn Irwin.

2003

Robert Clarence Irwin is born to Steve and Terri Irwin.

2010

Robert appears with sister Bindi in the movie *Free Willy: Escape from Pirate's Cove.*

2013

The *Robert Irwin: Dinosaur Hunter* book series is published.

2015

Robert makes a guest appearance on *Ten Deadliest Snakes.*

2016

The Australian Geographic Nature Photographer of the Year competition names Robert junior runner-up. He is a finalist in the competition in 2017, 2018, and 2019 too.

2017

Robert makes his first appearance on *The Tonight Show Starring Jimmy Fallon.*

2018

Robert and Bindi win the Nickelodeon Kids' Choice award for Favorite Duo.

2020

Robert releases a 2020 calendar that features his wildlife photography.

QUIZ

#1

What do zoologists study?

#2

What is the purpose of
Wildlife Warriors?

#3

Who opened the Australia
Zoo in 1970?

#4

What animal does Robert
love the most?

#5

The Irwins' Animal Planet
show airs in how many
countries and territories?

#6

Which Kids' Choice award
did Robert and Bindi
win in 2018?

1. Wildlife and their natural habitats
2. To fund projects that help wild animals
3. Robert's grandparents, Bob and Lyn Irwin
4. The saltwater crocodile
5. More than 205
6. Favorite Duo

ACTIVITY

There are many endangered animals around the world. They could become extinct if people continue to hunt them or push them out of their native habitats. Conduct a research project on the importance of an endangered animal.

MATERIALS

- computer with internet access
- library access
- pencil and paper

STEPS

1. Choose one endangered animal.

2. Conduct research about that animal. Use the internet, books, and articles to find out about the ways the world will be affected by the animal's disappearance from the planet.

3. Find out if people are trying to help this animal. What is their approach? Is it working? What other ways can you come up with to help this animal?

4. Take notes about all your findings.

5. Use your notes to write a report. Present your report to your family, friends, or classmates.

GLOSSARY

advocate: to publicly support

ambassador: someone who represents a group while living in another country

conservation: the protection of something, such as animals and plants

controversy: strong disagreement about something

debut: the first time someone does something in public, such as appear on TV

ecosystem: everything that exists in a certain environment, including soil, rocks, water, plants, and animals

endangered: rare and in danger of dying out completely

expression: a word or phrase

extinct: when all the members of a species have died

food chain: a list of living things in which each one uses the lower member on the list as a source of food

habitat: a place where a plant or animal normally lives

homeschool: to learn at home instead of at a school

poach: to hunt illegally

service animal: an animal trained to assist a human who has a disability

species: a group of plants or animals with similar features

vital: very important

wildlife: animals living in the wild

READ MORE

Anastasio, Dina. *Who Was Steve Irwin?* New York: Penguin Workshop, 2015.

Cronin, Leonard. *The Australian Animal Atlas.* Crows Nest, New South Wales: Allen & Unwin, 2018.

Ignotofsky, Rachel. *The Wondrous Workings of Planet Earth: Understanding Our World and Its Ecosystems.* New York: Ten Speed Press, 2018.

Rice, William B. *Life and Non-Life in an Ecosystem.* Huntington Beach, CA: Teacher Created Materials, 2015.

INTERNET SITES

https://www.edumedia-sciences.com/en/node/51-ecosystems
Explore different types of ecosystems and the creatures that live in them.

http://species-in-pieces.com
Explore an exhibit about 30 endangered species.

https://www.australiazoo.com.au/support-wildlife/programs/
Find out about the conservation projects supported by the Australia Zoo and Irwin.

https://zoo.sandiegozoo.org/cams/koala-cam
Watch koalas in real time and learn more about them.

INDEX